Ten Fami...
in East Devon

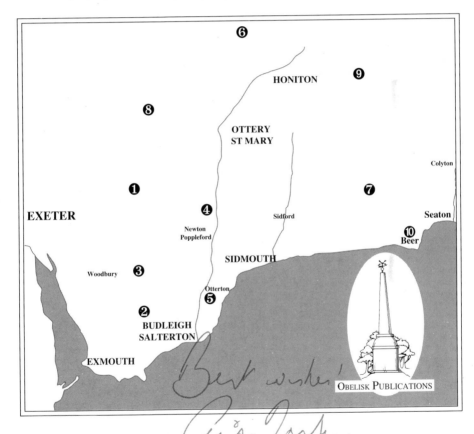

EXETER

HONITON

⑥

⑨

⑧

OTTERY
ST MARY

Colyton

①

④

⑦

Seaton

Newton
Poppleford

Sidford

⑩
Beer

Woodbury

③

SIDMOUTH

Otterton

⑤

②

BUDLEIGH
SALTERTON

EXMOUTH

OBELISK PUBLICATIONS

Best wishes!

Chips Barber.

Sally & Chips Barber

ALSO BY THE AUTHORS
Ten Family Walks on Dartmoor
Six Short Pub Walks on Dartmoor
Dark & Dastardly Dartmoor
Ghastly & Ghostly Devon
Weird & Wonderful Dartmoor
Haunted Pubs in Devon
The Ghosts of Exeter

OTHER 'WALKING' TITLES FROM OBELISK PUBLICATIONS INCLUDE:
Diary of a Dartmoor Walker, Chips Barber
Diary of a Devonshire Walker, Chips Barber
The Great Walks of Dartmoor, Terry Bound
Walking with a Tired Terrier In and Around Torbay, Brian Carter
Walks in the South Hams, Brian Carter
Pub Walks in the South Hams, Brian Carter
The Templer Way, Derek Beavis
Walks in the Shadow of Dartmoor, Denis McCallum
Walks in Tamar and Tavy Country, Denis McCallum
Walks in the Totnes Countryside, Bob Mann
Wheelchair Walks in Devon, Lucinda Ruth Gardner
The Dartmoor Mountain Bike Guide, Peter Barnes

We have over 100 Devon titles, for further details please send SAE to the address below or telephone (01392) 468556

At the time of publication all the walks in this book were mostly along paths designated as official footpaths or rights of way, but it should be borne in mind that diversion orders may be made from time to time, and the authors/publishers cannot accept responsibility for those who stray from the rights of way.

PLATE ACKNOWLEDGEMENTS
All sketch maps redrawn from an out-of-copyright source by Sally Barber
All photographs by Chips Barber apart from page 22 (top) by Pam Reynolds

First published in 1992
Reprinted in 1995 by
Obelisk Publications, 2 Church Hill, Pinhoe, Exeter, Devon
Designed by Chips and Sally Barber
Typeset by Sally Barber
Printed in Great Britain by
The Devonshire Press Limited, Torquay, Devon

INTRODUCTION

What is a 'family walk'? To us it is a walk capable of being completed by most age groups from medium small child (our youngest was eight at the time) up to active pensioner. In the interests of research we roped in various family members at different times, and they always concluded the walk by saying "If we can do it, anyone can!"

For this book we have included ten walks of varying length, but none more than five miles, enough to result in some healthy exercise without causing a mutiny in the junior (or senior) ranks! A useful ploy has been to tell would-be participants the distance of the walk in miles rather than kilometres. The thought of a four mile jaunt is less daunting than a slog of almost seven kilometres, even though it's the same distance! A little bit of kidology never hurt anybody.

One thing is guaranteed, and that is these walks are in some of the loveliest East Devon countryside. We searched out a mixture of surroundings so expect to encounter woodlands, lanes, fields, commons, rivers and coastline (but not necessarily on the same walk!).

Naturally with such a diverse range of terrain it is inevitable that wet conditions underfoot will be encountered occasionally. In order to minimise any discomfort it is always recommended that stout or waterproof footwear is worn at all times.

The sketch maps included only show a minimal amount of detail. It is recommended that you acquire the four Ordnance Survey "Pathfinder" 1:25 000 sheets which cover this area. These are Sheet No 1296 (Honiton and Cullompton), 1315 (Ottery St Mary), 1330 (Sidmouth) and 1316 (Lyme Regis and Axminster).

All the walks are circular so unless you have great trouble following simple instructions, you should never need to retrace your footsteps. Wherever you start, you finish – hopefully!

This book follows hard-on-the-heels of *Ten Family Walks on Dartmoor*, a book we are told has given a lot of pleasure to those who bought it. We hope that you too will enjoy these little outings as much as we did!

3

❶ Almost All Around Aylesbeare!

If it's possible to have a West of East Devon then Aylesbeare is just that! It lies on that broad shoulder of land that rises from the depression of the Exe basin. It is quiet country, so quiet in fact that professional people use it as a dormitory settlement, a retreat to retire to after the day-to-day dealings of their distant daily business life. But for us walkers it is both the starting and finishing point of a lovely little circular stroll of about three and a half miles.

The starting point is as close to Aylesbeare Church as it is possible to park with room for an occasional car to park near the church's lych gate. On a Sunday there will obviously be competition from churchgoers!

Enter the churchyard where a signpost indicates a public footpath which leads to the right of the church. If you have difficulty, because of your bulk, in negotiating this kissing gate, or the one at the north west side of the church yard, you can console yourself that the walk will burn off some calories! The gateway to the countryside was in a sad state of affairs when we did this walk – two leaning towers of brick heading towards each other!

Ahead lies an open rolling countryside of fields and stiles and even more stiles! In fact on this walk we even found a stile without anything for it to be a stile for – a lonely object which demanded attention. Quite probably a high percentage of people feel sorry for it like we did and climb it for posterity – that one though

was a field away. It lies just beyond our first obstacle across the field to the north west and is easily reached. The next stile presents no problem other than a mild dilemma. Here two footpath signs point in differing directions.

To stay with this walk you have to observe the left one which appears to send you off across the field into 'no man's land'. However if you follow its general direction towards a distant gateway, you will ultimately discover another stile –

which of course you will take in your stride and vault with all the accomplishment of a seasoned walker. Failing that you will deposit yourself in the dampness beyond it. The way ahead is a doddle! A hedge on your left should be followed in surroundings where the views have opened up considerably.

Beyond Exeter, to the right of the geometrically designed rooftops of Sowton Estate, can be spied the distant satellite tracking beacon of Waddles Down above Whitestone. To the left and above the industrial estate rises the heights of Dartmoor with Cawsand Beacon, Yes Tor and Dartmoor's highest point High Willhays all clearly visible (on a good day). If it appears to be fine for you and cloudy out over the moors you can gloat over your wisdom to walk in an area of Devon which boasts far lower rainfall figures than its highest moorlands. If you can't see the hills then it is probably raining there!

Whilst musing over our own good fortune we reach the next stile. To the left and beyond the gateway is a small pond but we continue on down a slight slope to the next

To Exeter Airport

AYLESBEARE

(Lots of stiles)

Rosamondford House

Perkin's Village

(A damp lane)

To Sidmouth and Lyme Regis

To EXETER + Crealy Country

A3052

gateway. The way ahead is not clear at first. Ahead you will see a house and to your right a hedge. If you head towards the hedge, by steering right of the house, a camouflaged footpath sign and stile will be located. This leads onto the road where we turn left.

Rosamondford Lodge and the entrance to the house will soon be passed. It is a thought that anyone who died in this small hamlet may well have been carried to burial along the path we have just followed as it was customary to take the most direct route and these are long standing routes – let's hope that didn't have as many stiles to negotiate.

In spring time this section of the lane is a riot of flowers. The ford at Rosamondford enables passing cars an occasional splash after heavy rain but a neat footbridge spares the wayfarer an unwanted baptism. The stream, for some obscure reason, is referred to as The Rags but is usually just a trickle. Just beyond is the picturesque Rosamondford Farm with its thatched, detached entrance porch – resembling a lych gate. Outside of it is an unusual post box and opposite is the detached, but extended, Ford Cottage. Yards away a yellow arrow is accompanied by a sign, which states that: "This public right of way has been diverted by statutory order. Please follow the way marked route." So do!

Continue past the aptly-named Brook Cottage and almost opposite the next terrace of cottages turn left, climb a few steps to mount the stile and enter the field. After the muddy gateway, walk up beside the right hand hedge, and after 60 yards cross another stile. In front of you, and up the slope, is the next destination, a metal gate some 200 yards ahead.

The next stile is not visible from this point but lies in the only exit to the next field, in the same general direction, about 200 yards further on. When it is reached a small pond will be also be evident just to the right – a newt's paradise. This stile was dangerously rickety when we encountered it so if it hasn't improved by the time you arrive, tread with care! Another one awaits within 30 yards. Cross this and its accompanying damp dip then walk up to the road.

On reaching it, continue on the same line for about 40 yards. A muddy track continues whilst the road bears right but a footpath pointing into the field gives the next point of direction for this ramble. A long, narrowish field rises, at first gently, from this point. Follow the left hand hedge which climbs steadily upwards to a stile in the field's top left hand corner. Carry on with the hedge on your left. The extra glucose sweets or Kendal mint cake are useful now as a few miles have been covered and ahead lies the only unpleasant part of the walk – unless of course you relish a challenge.

At the next stile the open fields give way to a newer stile which heads into a lane. This can be a muddy affair and it is quite easily the muddiest section of the walk. We were disfigured by some prickly and thorny vegetation which had been felled across this muddy track. In reality the lane is not all that long – it just seems that way – leading to Lower Nutwalls. As the junction is approached the ground beneath becomes ever firmer whilst the road to the left, to Randlehayes Farm, is a much drier thoroughfare which we follow.

Ahead can be seen the tower of Aylesbeare Church. Opposite the main buildings at Randlehayes Farm a footpath heads right to yet another stile which, we suppose, helps to make this a steeplechase rather than a race on the flat. Beyond it lies a line of expensive-looking detached houses, the sort where the double garages themselves would make a reasonable sized home. Between them is a gap, which will head onto the road.

It's all downhill stuff now back to your vehicle; the former primary school and the pub are distinct landmarks as the walk wearily drops itself to a conclusion and a well earned rest.

This walk is off the beaten track – when we did it we saw more rabbits, squirrels and deer than we did people, making it a very pleasant way to spend about one and a half hours.

❷ Delightful Dalditch

If you ever compare maps of Woodbury's many commons with reality you will discover that it can be the most confusing mismatch. It is possible to get totally lost without really trying too hard! On this three mile adventure, hopefully our instructions will guide you through the maze.

The starting point is at the car park near Squabmoor Reservoir. This can be reached from the B3179 Woodbury to Budleigh Salterton road, at its junction with St John's Road, by taking a smaller road which heads north eastwards towards East Budleigh Common. Fencing lines the left of this road with glimpses of Bystock Reservoir visible between the trees on the left side. After about a half mile the road starts to climb steeply and a car park beneath pine trees is clearly identifiable on the right side of the road. Park here (grid ref 038 844).

The start of the walk involves walking a very short distance north eastwards along the road to its first curve. Here is a stumpy, fat little pine tree, beside which is the start of a track. Its beginning is almost concealed but after its first sharp bend right, then left, there is an obvious corridor to follow and, unlike many on or around the Woodbury Common area, it is not too hard on the feet. The many hoof marks on the ground is evidence that it is a popular thoroughfare for horse riders. So be warned that any sounds of distant galloping hooves is very likely to be the real thing rather than a group of sound effects people using coconut shells just to fool you!

At the first junction ignore the track going right and downhill, and continue straight on. Stay on this main track which leads downhill to a fork. The left branch should be selected. Proof that the route instructions have been followed correctly is the sight of a distant flat topped hill – straight ahead – which is crowned with telegraph poles (do we hear a cheer?).

Proceed straight ahead and don't be persuaded otherwise. In a short while a gateway with a stile presents itself. Don't cross but steer left with the track for it soon broadens out into a pleasant corridor between an avenue of trees. To the left is 'common' whilst to the right are fields.

After several hundred yards a country version of a 'roundabout' is encountered. Downhill from the left a broad track emerges and ahead our track continues for about another 40 yards. From here, turn immediately right onto a track which has fields on both sides. This track, which has a few squelchy short sections, is with

us for about half a mile. Its hedges are home to a variety of critters.

Eventually when the brow of a hill is reached, three yellow direction markers will be seen on a gate – two appear to give sensible alternatives for walkers to follow whilst the third presents an impossible option – straight up! As it is not our intention to head heavenwards just yet, stay with the lane for a while longer. At the next brow it is possible to spy, again straight ahead, the club house of Budleigh Salterton's East Devon golf course. Either side of that and beyond is the sea.

The lane which has roller-coastered gently so far now drops down quite steeply. At a gateway in a snake-like bend the very distinctive Georgian Tidwell House can be spotted away to the east. Believed to be haunted, this is now a hotel.

At this point the track splits again. Take the right fork which bends downhill. In this sunken lane there are large exposures of the new red sandstone rocks so common in East Devon. Several folk have etched their names and messages onto the exposure but an amazing, equally exposed, tree which grows high on the right side of the lane looks precariously placed. It gives new meaning to the phrase 'standing under a tree' as the track goes right below it, giving an extraordinary view of its root system.

The lane ends at a junction by Dalditch Apiary (which means a home for bees – not apes!). Although the walk's route dictates a right turn here, it is well to point out to railway buffs that just down the road to the left can be seen an impressive bridge which once (probably more than once!) carried the trains on the Budleigh Salterton to Exmouth line.

The road will only need to be followed for about 200 yards as opposite Dalditch Stables another clear track leads off to the right. A signpost by the gateway confirms that it is fine to proceed. This next section is about the steepest 'up' section of the walk but it is not too demanding and leads to more open 'common' type country again which is more level!

Just beyond a triangular shaped piece of open land on the right, stay with the main track until an obvious fork is reached, ignoring the one which snakes off to the right.

Take the left hand fork and after about another one hundred yards repeat the manoeuvre again. This one leads to Squabmoor Reservoir's sloped dam wall. It is more than likely that after seeing only an occasional walker, now a relative crowd will be milling around enjoying the scenic splendour of this attractive small reservoir which is noted for its coarse fishing.

It is possible to walk the entire circumference of the lake. The west bank is wooded and to walk that side would complete a Dalditch trio – Dalditch Apiary, Dalditch Stables and now Dalditch Plantation. It is somewhat surprising that the reservoir is not called Dalditch Reservoir – perhaps that choice of name was thought to be as 'dull as ditch' water? The east bank provides an equally level path and indeed a shorter distance route back towards the starting point of the walk.

At the end of the reservoir continue on the natural line of the main track in a NNW direction. The other people probably drifting back to their cars will act as unwitting guides should there be any confusion. In no time vehicles will be seen playing a half-hearted version of hide and seek amongst the pine trees from where the walk commenced.

For the record, we ambled around in under one and a half hours despite stopping to make copious notes in the process. It was an enjoyable romp and we hope you don't get lost!

❸ A Walk on Wonderful Woodbury Common

This is another little walk in the Woodbury Common area, one which features some of its better-known landmarks. The starting point is most easily reached from the B3180 road which crosses these East Devon commons. Turn eastwards at Pine Ridge (023 844) along a minor road which skirts the southern edge of Lympstone Common.

All the various commons fall under the umbrella heading of Woodbury Common, probably because many of them are very small and it is difficult to see where one begins and another ends! For the record there is East Budleigh, Lympstone, Shortwood, Dalditch, Colaton Raleigh, Bicton, Aylesbeare, Harpford, Venn Ottery and Woodbury Common somewhere in the middle of all of them.

About a mile along this road, beyond a car park on the left, is a choice of car parks. On the right is one which has a building which resembles a garage at its entrance, whilst opposite is another which may be a better choice as this three and a half to four mile walk starts and ends in it.

We are at or near 'Fryingpans' which, bearing in mind one of the names on the cover of this book, would seem to be an appropriate location from which to begin a walk!

Walk through the car park – a signed marker post with a blue arrow indicates the way to proceed for the time being. Very soon an enormous quarry will be visible to the left of this extremely wide thoroughfare. It would be an excellent location for sci-fi film-makers to use as a Martian landscape – it is redder even than The Red Planet itself! However these are lovely surroundings and it is unlikely that any Martians will escape the confines of the barbed wire fence which keeps out would-be trespassers whilst ensuring that the rambler stays on the 'straight and wide' (as opposed to the 'straight and narrow') which lies ahead.

On the right is a coniferous plantation which gives way to a track leading to the right. Ignore this and walk downhill. Ahead a pond will be visible in the bottom of the quarry – The Red Lagoon? At the bottom of this pleasant slope is a fork in the paths. It is simply a case of putting off the inevitable! Instead of tackling the steeper slope immediately ahead, it is probably better to branch left along a track which has suffered from that geographical phenomenon called gully erosion. All the loose material has been washed downhill so make sure that you don't suffer the same fate!

The top of the slope is soon reached. (Notice how it is not referred to as a hill. A hill would render you more breathless!) With that as a small consolation, the way lies straight ahead between conifers.

A quarter mile ahead is Four Firs which is the next destination. To its right, and above it, is the large clump of trees which conceals Woodbury Castle.

Four Firs is easily reached as the track makes a bee-line for it. Walk through the car park to the crossroads. Look up the road towards the castle and a public bridleway signpost will be seen about 50 yards along the road on the left hand side. Initially it is better to be on the right hand verge for a short way before crossing in good time to avoid a blind bend. Turn left onto this track which becomes one of the most pleasant sections of this four-mile ramble.

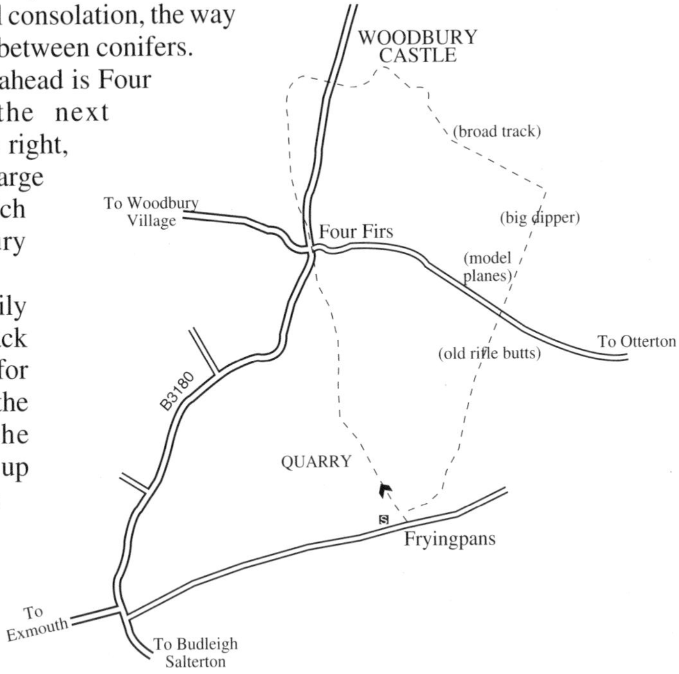

This bridleway, with views over Woodbury village, across the Exe estuary to the Haldon Hills and beyond to Dartmoor's dizzy heights, descends to wend its way at the base of the Bunter Pebble scarp. The geological divide between this common-type land and the grassy fields is clearly apparent. This track is one of the less stony ones of the district, which is just as well as it is followed for several hundred yards. Despite the fact that the busy road runs on the ridge high above, this is a quiet route which is stayed with until the first obvious fork is encountered.

Here all sorts of possibilities present themselves but we fork right to climb the hill towards the woods of Woodbury Castle at the top, ignoring the two wickedly stony tracks down from the right. Just before the road is reached, a tiny disused quarry will be seen on the right.

WOODBURY CASTLE

(broad track)

To Woodbury Village

Four Firs

(big dipper)

(model planes)

(old rifle butts)

To Otterton

B3180

QUARRY

Fryingpans

To Exmouth

To Budleigh Salterton

11

Cross the B3180 road to enter the car park where a band of wooden stumps cleverly prevent motorists from intruding onto the common. If young children are on this ramble they will, no doubt, summon up hidden reserves of energy to romp about all over this Iron-Age hill fort. It also saw activity in Roman times as Alauna Sylva, and in Napoleonic times when a vigilant eye was kept on English Channel areas to see that our French chummies did not slip in unchallenged.

It is necessary to skirt the perimeter of this great, but unofficial, children's playground. Head around the south side of the castle defences ignoring the first track to the right until an obvious gap in the wall and moat reveals a path coming from it. Turn 90 degrees right here and head for a hundred yards between a plantation of young conifers to reach another break in a hedge at the end of a line of tall trees.

To the left is another broad corridor fringed, on the left, by the line of trees. Turn left and walk for about 50 yards; on the right a wide track will be seen going a little back on itself. Take this track, which is soon joined by one from the right, and it will lead you away from the castle, downhill.

It is now extremely wide and those with extra thick soles on their footwear will reap the rewards as the going underfoot is somewhat hard. To all intents and purposes, the surrounding landscape is now one of rolling moorlands and on a misty/hazy day Woodbury and all its adjacent commons can seem quite desolate even though the uncultivated area is only about a mile wide at its widest point. Almost half a mile down the hill a double wide roller-coaster of a track leads away in a generally southwards direction. It can be easily located by turning right towards the bottom of the slope.

In real terms the forest which has loomed up in front of you is to be ignored in favour of this track which skirts it for quite a way. The big dipper that you encounter is not too demanding and the angle that your body inclines to scale the sharp rise enables you to have a close scrutiny of these rounded pebbles, once the bed of an enormous river which used to flow from France (long before Napoleon was a twinkle in his father's eye). Beyond is a straightish track with a gentle gradient.

This is a kingdom of recreational pursuits, in particular model aeroplane enthusiasts can often be seen indulging in the art of guiding sophisticated flying machines, which sound like liberated lawnmowers, over this part of the common. You might also encounter the Royal Marines (dressed up like the vegetation), horse riders, other walkers, joggers, mountain bikers, or orienteerers who charge from obstacle to obstacle with mazed determination! We will pursue our stroll with leisurely disdain.

In another quarter of a mile a damp depression is reached, with a group of trees ahead. Ignoring other paths, head for these trees where there is a car park with, should they be needed, several benches on which to sit for a breather.

Leave this car park by the vehicular exit; immediately opposite will be spotted a well-worn, but narrow, track into yet another car park. Go straight on downhill to a point where there are the remains of a probable set of targets, shown as old firing butts on six inch maps. The way ahead is not too obvious, so walk down over the scarred, red hillside until you see a small stream which has a man-made dam-like obstruction across it. Go down to this and sidestep, in your own dainty style, any overtly wet terrain.

From this point an obvious straight path leads slightly downhill; this should be followed as to wander from it will almost certainly guarantee a very wet baptism which will not be appreciated with just half a mile to go! Because of the nature of Woodbury Common's geology surface streams are rare. They are only found when valleys have been cut down to the underlying marls. These retain the water and form valley bogs, like the ones of distant Dartmoor. This damp depression is a fine example of this geological occurrence. Another stream is met after about 200 yards.

Ahead is a slope, at the top of which is a flight of steps. Steer just left of them and continue until a crossroads of tracks is reached. Turn right then almost immediately left! Initially this drops into a shallow dip but soon rises to form a prolonged climb. Never fear, for after rising to negotiate a dog-leg the path arrives back at the path which started us off earlier. Where it rejoins there are two stone tablets resembling, we would imagine, The Ten Commandments. Alas they bear no such edicts so turn left and your vehicle should soon be reached.

❹ In And Around the Otter Valley

Harpford, a picture postcard-type village in the Otter Valley, is the starting point for this lovely walk of about 4 miles. Like so many villages in this valley, Harpford is wisely located just above the flood plain of the River Otter.

There is room for a few cars to park just below the church where the road is a little wider. There is even a bench strategically located so that you can go through that familiar ritual of donning your walking boots or shoes without resorting to the 'hopping around on one leg' dance that is so comical to behold.

As a point of interest, Augustus Toplady was once, for a dozen or so years, the local vicar. He is noted for writing the well-known hymn 'Rock of Ages'. The churchyard cross is a memorial to him.

Our walk begins by strolling away from the church in the direction of the river. On the bend of the road a footpath is signposted to the right. Follow it and in a short distance another sign indicates the way to a footbridge spanning the Otter. Cross the footbridge and keep on straight across the field where the path is discernible.

The next stile was probably installed by a giant because it makes little allowance for people with short inside leg measurements!

A series of bright yellow arrows are located as straight ahead remains the flavour of the day. The third footbridge, which is soon encountered, creates the first real opportunity to take the wrong route. Cross this bridge and two yellow arrows offer a choice. Take the set of steps which go to the right!

For a while the narrow path runs along the side of the hill in wooded surroundings until a stile leads into a field. By heading right this public right of way will lead you to another stile at the bottom of the field. Beyond it the track is then enclosed by hedges. Simply stay with the yellow arrows and the bends will not cause any doubts as to your intended destination.

After about 300 easy yards the lane is left in favour of a steeper uphill climb up the left side of a long narrow field. On this climb it is possible to gaze back on Harpford or glimpse in the opposite direction Harpford Common, crowned with a tall lonesome pine (the Exeter-Sidmouth road passes within yards of it).

A stile is concealed in the top left corner and marks yet another 90 degree manoeuvre. Follow the edge of the hedge to the umpteenth stile and follow the green lane up to the road junction at Lynch Head. Turn right over the brow of the hill and drop down to Venn Ottery, which is cosily nestled in a tributary valley of the Otter.

The oldest building in Venn Ottery is the church which has a tower dating back to about 1100. However the rest of the building is much newer as a fire in the eighteenth century ravaged this hamlet. A smithy, an inn and several cottages were destroyed.

At the crossroads by the hotel and Barton Mews take the track, just to the left of the signpost, which leads steadily uphill. Although it is a bit of a climb, it is well worthwhile as at the top, beside the stout stump of a stalwart tree, marooned on a triangular island of grass, you will be rewarded with a great view. Up the valley is Ottery St. Mary and distant Hembury hill fort, whilst to the north west is upmarket Westhill – delightfully hidden from sight by equally exclusive designer trees!

But we are at a T-junction and decisions have to be made. Turn right then, after about 50 yards, turn left onto the signposted public bridleway. This is a soft thoroughfare made even softer by the shovellable evidence deposited by passing through horses! Soon the bridleway drops sharply down to civilisation. Go left of the houses, which constitute some of the hamlet of Metcombe. Cross the road and head straight ahead.

After about 70 yards the road veers right and degenerates into a rough track which ascends the hill. Follow this track which soon shows itself to be an excellent choice as it has mild gradients, is gentle on those poor overused feet, and is great on the eye with panoramic views.

But all good lanes come to an end and this one is no exception as, after several hundred yards, it is met from the left by a steep track that plunges down North Hill. Turn right to walk down to the road which is only a few hundred yards away.

The thatched farm is Mountstephen Farm which, by turning right onto the road, you will almost circumnavigate. Follow the road southwards for about 200 yards and then turn left onto a signposted footpath. Proceed along it and pass through a wooden gate. A little further on is a metal gate; by using the adjacent stile you can save yourself two pounds for not leaving the gate ajar!

The raised embankment is the old trackbed of the former railway which ran from

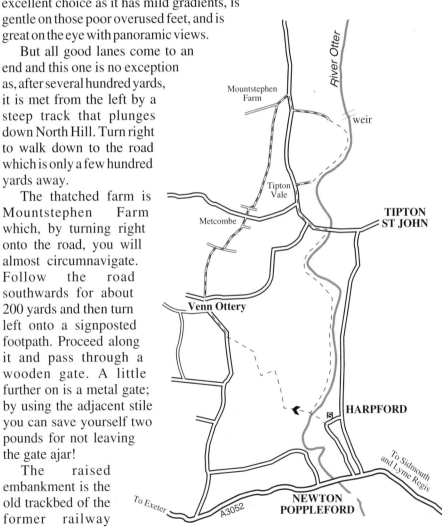

15

Sidmouth Junction (Feniton) down the Otter Valley to Budleigh Salterton then on to Exmouth. A branch just to the south of Tipton St. John fed Sidmouth with its own route.

If you feel so inclined, a waterfall off to the left makes a pleasant detour but if time is pressing walk downstream along the right bank of the Otter. An old mill

will be spotted on the opposite side of the river, a reminder of the days when water power reigned supreme. By staying with the river, a bend will be negotiated, the Otter appearing to become a dual carriageway for a short while as it approaches the five arched railway viaduct spanning the river. Do not cross but continue along the same side until a gateway is reached.

On passing through the gate, cross the small concrete footbridge and head between an avenue of trees on a very green, but not clearly obvious, path which leads to the right of the nearby houses of Tipton Vale. Turn left and remember to reduce your walking speed to under 30 mph!

Make your way towards Tipton St. John, ignoring the two possible roads to the right. A cunningly concealed pavement initially helps but a little road walking is required. Just before the bridge over the Otter at Tipton, a public footpath leads off on the west bank (to your right).

Take this path all the way along the Otter. You will be able to stay on this bank for a mile and route directions are unnecessary – provided that you identify Harpford with its "Rock of all Ages" church. Recross the footbridge, and the lane with bonus stiles, to get safely and soundly back to your vehicle.

❺ An Otterton Outing

The pretty-as-a-picture village of Otterton, justly proud of its appearance having done well in competitions like "The Best Kept Village", is the starting point for this extremely pleasant walk of about three to four miles. The village lies in a steep depression formed by the Otterton Brook, which trickles in a man-made channel beside the main street. The River Otter flows almost at a right angle to Otterton's general alignment.

Most people will probably approach the village from the direction of the A376 road which runs down the west side of the Otter Valley, turning off this road at Brick Cross. Cross the bridge which spans the disused track of a railway line and the bridge over the Otter. Park on the left-hand side beside the village sign and Victorian standpipe, which was re-erected here by local venture scouts in 1989 having previously been of service in Ottery St. (This is not a mistake – this is a road so does not need a 'Mary' to complete it!)

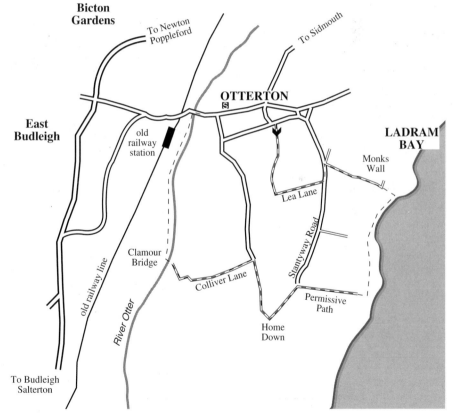

Walk up the main street, Fore St., away from Otterton Mill, go past the King's Arms, the bakery and the village store. At the top of the street turn right into Lea Road; a nameplate on the wall is clear but for further confirmation the farm on the junction with the road that goes on to Ladram Bay is Cross Tree Farm. There

17

are a few more houses around it now than when it was built!

Head uphill until a T-junction is reached at the unusual sounding 'Behind Hayes'. Turn left but in a matter of just a few yards turn right onto what is initially a gently rising green lane. Treat the ever-steepening gradient as a test of your stamina and fitness! Fortunately the path soon levels out and you can start to enjoy the walk again. Through several gateways on your right you may espy the obelisk at Bicton, plus the wood which caps Woodbury Common whilst concealing Woodbury Castle, also the church at East Budleigh is readily identifiable.

Eventually a more distinct track enters on a bend from the right. Head straight ahead which we suppose is technically left! In a short distance the path veers sharply to the left and continues between low banks, offering shelter on a windy day to very short people (or children) but for the taller element the reward is reasonable views of features like High Peak which is the triangular shaped hill ahead and to the left.

With the sea gleaming bright to the right, the end of the track is reached at another T-junction. Turn left. A little way ahead is a bench together with a sign indicating that the public right-of-way to the coast path is to the right. Ignoring all other route alternatives, go down the No Through Road which soon ends at Monks Wall Cottage, an idyllic spot. We steer to the right of it into a short lane which culminates with a stile. Cross it and proceed down the right-hand hedge of the field towards the sea.

Away to the left the East Devon Heritage Coast stretches impressively from the giant red sandstone sea stacks, which stand sentinel at Ladram Bay, past the popular Jacob's Ladder, along Sidmouth's sedate esplanade and beyond to the great white bastion-like cliff of Beer Head in the distance. Geologically this view ranges from the relatively predictable red sandstone cliffs, which erode in a more uniform fashion, to ones which might come tumbling down at any time! With such views and such thoughts to ponder we arrive at the coastal path on top of the cliffs. Go right towards "Budleigh Salterton", a name synonymous with veterans in bath robes plunging into the sea for their daily constitutional, P.G. Wodehouse and sketches from 'Monty Python'.

For the next quarter of a mile or so ignore any alternative unsigned routes and stay on the coast path. Notice as you go how the cliff-top vegetation has been blown for so long in the same direction that all the bushes and small trees rigidly incline the same way. Although there are numerous examples of the same phenomenon found in exposed and windy locations like North Devon and North Cornwall, here the vegetation is so shaped and sculptured by onshore sea breezes, not the prevailing south-westerlies like Celtic counterparts!

A stile is thus reached and a T-junction of alternatives is duly confronted. Most other walking books will now lead you ever onward to the mouth of the Otter – this is almost a convention! However we have the family to consider and we do not want to grind them into the dust so, to keep within a budget of four miles, we turn right onto a "Permissive Way" – a route provided by The East Devon Heritage Coast Service by kind permission of The Clinton Devon Estates. Signs and notices convey these details at this location.

This path leads down to a barn with two stiles (one at either end) and then has a burst of yellow arrows to take you past a South West Water installation (lovely!). At the end of this track another choice sees us turn left onto the signposted route to the "River Otter". This lane is Stantyway Lane and takes us to a gateway below Home Down. Beyond the gate veer right – you won't have any choice as other alternatives are on private land. Follow the lane down to Colliver Cross where you will find the signpost in the right-hand hedge trying to hide from you! Here the way to go is left down Colliver Lane, a tree-lined narrow path, very prettily flanked with celandines in spring when we walked along, making for an easy and pleasant few hundred yards.

A gathering of gateways is encountered but the way ahead is again obvious as a chicane and a bend around a field lead to the end of this track, culminating at a stile with a gate beside two large brick pillars. We recommend you use the stile as the evil little gate lever snapped on one of our family's fingers and inflicted a wound that was discussed for some time!

Walk between the pillars and immediately turn right to descend the steps to cross the bridge over the Otter. This is 'Clamour Bridge', most certainly not a 'Glamour Bridge' as its metal form is functional rather than decorative. Possibly 'Clamour' may derive its name from the rooks which live in the trees lining the Otter as 'clamour' is a collective name for them, not a glamorous bird either!

Now we are in the land of the common people (no disrespect meant) as the green meadows by the Otter are walked by many who simply like a straightforward, no-risks, no-adventure type outing. The way back to Otterton is right at Clamour Bridge then along the banks of the river.

When Otterton looms up its fine church stands boldly up on a high bluff of almost orange New Red Sandstone. Indeed there are some of the finest red river cliffs in Devon along this stretch. Opposite is the old railway station, now a private residence. It was, perhaps surprisingly, East Budleigh Station as it was on the west bank of the Otter. The railway line which passed through it linked Sidmouth Junction (Feniton) with Exmouth. It was a completed as a through route

in 1903. However, when the line was but 64 years old, it closed – in March 1967.

Now we are back in Otterton; depending on the time of day or the season it may be possible to get refreshments at Otterton Mill or the local pub. Failing that, it's home for a well-earned cup of tea!

❻ A Little Hike in the Hills – Broadhembury

Broadhembury must be one of the prettiest villages in Devon. It takes its name from the prominent hill fort of Hembury which is on a spur of high land above the village, and lies almost a mile to the east of the A373 Cullompton to Honiton road. As it is about five miles to the north west of Honiton it is, for us, in this book about as far north in East Devon as we dare go. The steep slopes of the hills above the village mark the southern limit of the Blackdown Hills which straddle the Devon/Somerset border.

Park in the centre of the village, which is a large open space complete with pub, post office and bench – a useful place on which to sit to don your boots. The Drewe Arms is named after a local family who lived at the Grange, just south west of the village. Edward Drewe, a highly successful Elizabethan lawyer bought it to add to his other Devon estates of Sharpham, high above the Dart near Totnes, and Killerton at Broadclyst.

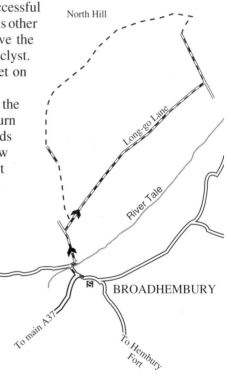

But enough of the history – let's get on with this lovely three mile walk.

Head away from the church towards the bridge. Cross the bridge or ford and turn right past the playground. The road bends sharp left but goes gently uphill. Follow the road to the right by the lone pine, just before the thatched cottage called 'Woodbine'. We are still going uphill as we pass the public footpath sign. Keep on up the hill, staying on the road, avoiding the track on the right.

After about 400 yards of gently going uphill, leave the surfaced road. Follow the public bridleway, which is technically right or straight ahead. Go through the gate with a sign warning that the fencing on the farm is electrified to 5,000 volts, enough to make sure that we stay on the track!

At the top of the hill you might see gliders over the trees. The ground will probably be a bit wet where you cross the stream, but it dries out as you start going up, with a green grassy area up the middle. At the T-junction turn left and you start going even steeper uphill. Head towards the caravans peeping over the skyline, with the stream gurgling in the ditch on your right hand side.

It was at about this point, half way up the steep gradient, that 'Grandad' regretted having three pints of beer and a turkey dinner before setting out on the walk! There is an opportunity to pause in the gateway where the stream crosses the track, to see the views of the steep slope of Hembury Hill fort across the valley.

This was a good idea because around the bend is the steepest section! With pine trees on the left, gorse on the right, turn round at this point and, straight through the gap, you might see distant Hay Tor in the distance.

At the top of the track, there is a stile on the left. Again draw breath if necessary, then cross the stile and walk towards the barn which actually turns out to be a hangar.

Now you are standing on a rough road. Turn left and walk along this road with caravans on your left and the airfield on your right until the track peters out. Keep going in the same direction, keeping to the left of three trees standing in open parkland on the right.

When you reach a penned in area, near the top of North Hill, keep it to your left until you come across several blue arrows on the fence. Go through the gateway, downhill for about 100 yards to a metal gateway, staying with the blue arrows. On the edge of an airstrip like this, we did muse over whether 'Red Arrows' might not have been more appropriate?

Foliage permitting, you should now get good views down to Broadhembury with the church of St Andrew's a dominant landmark. It was here that the Rev Augustus Montague Toplady saw out his days, being vicar here from 1768 – 1778. His 'Rock of Ages' hymn was written when he was a priest in Somerset.

Go through another gate and, in the right season, you will be greeted by a carpet of bluebells or foxgloves. When the path opens out, keep the open field to the left and head towards the track – a blue arrow shows the way down the hill. In a fairly short distance there is a stile to the left with a yellow arrow on the left.

Cross the stile and looking down the line of the hedge in the distance you should be able to see Belvedere Tower on the Haldon Hills with Hay Tor (another Rock of all Ages) behind and to the right on the skyline. Diagonally to your right you now cross the field to another yellow arrow on a stile. Hop over the stile into the wood, then after about 50 yards you come across another stile out of the wood into a field.

Cross a small 'bridge' and proceed keeping the hedge on the left. Halfway down the field you can see Woodbury Castle on the horizon to the SSE.

At the bottom of the field there is another stile marked Public Footpath which takes us down a short lane with a metal gate at the end. There is no stile here but it's easy to cross the fence if you have long legs.

A short track enters a field. Cross it in the middle towards a further stile with a yellow arrow. There is a good view of the church so head generally towards it.

A stile at the bottom of the field will soon become obvious. This last mile or so has compensated for the first one which was almost all uphill. The cows in this last field were obviously not too used to walkers intruding on their privacy. All of them, to a cow, came across to say 'how do'. Stalwart members of our family showed a neat turn of pace at this point. The one who reached the stile first, vaulting it in record time, declared that had the herd charged, she could have captured the event on video! Fortunately, however, just how close they would have come we shall never know as a small ditch acted as a convenient moat between us.

Safe on the sanctuary of the road, turn right and head downhill back to the village where the large gardens at the rear of Broadhembury's main street are a scene of much activity in fine weather. However, it's not green fingers, but muddy boots which concern us most. Luckily the ford by the bridge, provided the river is not in spate, is ideal for cleaning any mud from your boots, thereby making that particular chore less of a task to do later and also reducing the amount of mud (and other country substances) to be transported home in your car.

❼ Back to the Iron Age – A Ramble to Blackbury Castle

The "Three Horse Shoes" is on the A3052 Exeter-Lyme Regis road about half way between Sidford and Colyford. The pub is run by Mr and Mrs Moore who have kindly consented for walkers wishing to do this two and a half to three mile walk to park in their car park, a gesture we greatly appreciate.

Walk along the main road, in the Sidford direction, towards the junction but stay on the verge as it is a very busy road. Before reaching the junction turn right onto a track towards a house. The track swings left of the house, then goes to the left of some farm outbuildings.

Go through the gate and away from the farm along a hedge-lined track. When the track makes an obvious fork, head right, downhill, through the wood. At the right time of year, this wood is a mass of bluebells. Keep on downhill, ignoring the track on the left, until you reach the shallow ford or stream at the bottom.

This is where what went downhill, now goes up! Walk on, straight ahead, slightly right. The path becomes slightly steeper then even more steep but it will level out eventually! Keep straight on to the top of the track where there is a metal gate. Turn right at the metalled road and pass the track to Little Farm.

Almost immediately we reach Blackbury Camp on the right. A well-worn track runs along the 'ramparts' which children will probably prefer to walking on the road. It is named

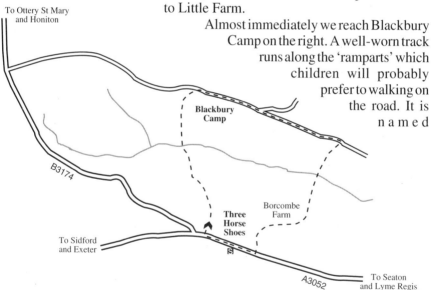

Blackbury Castle on the map but is signed Blackbury Camp – perhaps a misnomer as the sign also says 'no camping'! It is one of many iron-age forts found in East Devon. It dates to one or two centuries before Christ in the days when there was great rivalry between the predominantly Devonshire tribe of the Dumnonii and the equally barbarous tribe of the Durotriges from Dorset. Their main form of weaponry was sling shot; mounds of stones have been found in the cluster of hill forts which span the high spots of East Devon.

Keep on down the metalled road through the trees. At Southleigh Hill Cross keep on the same road (right) for another 500 yards. Ignore any unsignposted tracks into woods. Keep on until you leave the woods. Just as you leave the wooded area you get a good view of Borcombe Wood on the right through the gateway. Although this is a section of road walking, it is generally a quiet thoroughfare.

Pass Sailing-light Farm – ahead you will soon see a Public Footpath sign pointing right and left. We want to go right but when we walked here some barbed wire fencing made entry impossible! If you continue on the road for about 50 yards, on the right is a grassy track downhill for 100 yards to a crossroads of tracks. Turn right to follow the broad track downhill and across a stream beside a pond.

The track rises up the hillside towards the right. Go through the gate and turn left at a T-junction to go through another gate. Keep on the gently rising track, not the steep one on the right.

The track leads us through Borcombe Farm – which offers bed and breakfast

accommodation should you wish to make an overnight stay on this shortish walk! It angles off sharply to the right in front of the farmhouse. With stables on the right, take the left gateway, then follow the track at the base of a steep field on the left. The track peters out but head on towards a gate straight ahead. Go through the gate and follow the line of the hedge on the right.

At the top of the field, turn left to follow the hedge along the track well used by farm vehicles. You will reach the main road by a gate marked with a Public Footpath sign.

The car park and pub are back along the main road on your right – once again, use the wide verge as it is a very busy road! The Three Horse Shoes warmly welcomes children and has an inviting outdoor play area for those with any energy left, so if you need refreshment, you know where to go!

❽ A Short Walk in Cider Country

Whimple is the starting point for this one mile stroll. This lovely village lies a short distance from the A30 Exeter to Honiton road, about 9 miles from Devon's county town. For lovers of cider this is, or was, the heartland of this heady brew which gave the stereotyped Devon rustic his bright red rosy cheeks. The name of Whiteway was synonymous with cider production, for many years producing a wide variety of ciders. However we have come to walk in this kingdom of apple orchards so park in the village centre near St. Mary's Church.

A small stream runs down the street. Follow it for a short distance until a public footpath leads off to the right at Brook House. This takes you beside the scout hut then under the railway. This unattractive little lane leads to better things so don't worry, once you have skirted some relatively recent development, then crossed a few tiny footbridges, you will emerge onto a road where another public footpath permits you to go straight ahead.

A stile provides a little exercise as a field and pleasanter surroundings are encountered. Follow up the left side of this field which leads to another stile. Away to the west and to your left is a fine view. The ridge of the Haldon Hills is clearly evident with Belvedre Tower (Lawrence Castle) standing out as a distinct landmark. To the right of this, on the distant horizon, is Dartmoor. On a good day you may be able to identify Hay Tor, Hameldown Hill, or the peaks of such eminent hills as Whitehorse, Hangingstone and Cosdon.

All around are neat rows of cider apple trees. By entering the next gateway a short distance beyond the stile you will be amongst them! Keep the fence to your left and proceed through the orchard which, given the right time of year, would be an absolute picture. But all good things come to an end and, as the orchard rolls down the hill, a gateway beckons which will be easily reached through an avenue of trees. On reaching the road turn left and walk along it for about 250 yards. It is a reasonably straight section of road – if you keep to the right you will be able to continue without too much danger.

Hidden away from view on the left hand side is a signed public footpath which should be followed. It leads gently downhill to some buildings on the right. Just beyond them it becomes a metalled thoroughfare then, after twisting a little, Barnshayes will be seen on the right.

Soon this footpath ends – the way ahead lies to the right, under the very obvious railway tunnel not far away. Remember that if you are more than twelve feet six inches tall you should duck your head!

Bear left as soon as you have managed to negotiate this bridge. The way back to Whimple is all along this quiet lane. The Exeter-Waterloo line keeps you company on your left and the village is soon reached.

❾ A Woodland Walkabout at Offwell

Offwell is a lovely village not far from Honiton, just three quarters of a mile from the main Honiton to Axminster road, deriving its name from Offa's Well. There is space for a few vehicles to park at the junction by the fifteenth century church of St. Mary's.

This tiny village holds much of interest for the local historian; Les Garey's lively history of the parish, simply entitled "Offwell", reveals all!

We begin our walk with the words which are found inscribed on the school: 'The fear of the Lord is the beginning of wisdom'. However, the 'fear of the traffic' is a more practical concern as we head out of the village on the road towards Honiton which, of course, is quite possibly the way we arrived! Fortunately it is not a busy road, and there is generally good visibility and width to ameliorate any real danger.

The village shop is passed, then many attractive bungalows line the road as Offwell is soon left behind. On leaving the speed restricted area, a view of a tower presents itself ahead.

This tower, which has featured in several television programmes, was built at the behest of Edward Copleston who was born here in 1776. He succeeded his father as the vicar of Offwell, then went on to higher things when he became the Bishop of Llandaff in South Wales. There are those who say that his 80 feet tall tower was built so that he could look from its lofty summit all the way across country, over the Bristol Channel to Llandaff Cathedral (and presumably vice-versa!). Dream on!

Whilst these thoughts distract us, an ugly SWEB installation is passed on the right, partly masked by some pretty scruffy conifers. On the next bungalow is an unusual weather vane which will appeal to those who are equine orientated.

Literally yards before the junction with the main road, a minor road leads off to the left towards Bluebell Farm. Follow this lane – it is the closest we will get to the tower, in fact in a short distance we will lose sight of it completely. On the left a deep chasm appears which holds the Offwell Brook, a steep gully eroded by the stream in torrent times. Stay on this road until a choice of route is offered near Bluebell Farm. Resist the option proposed by the footpath sign.

Continue with the track which has the antique charm of a scrap metal yard on your left – contemporary modern art? Go through the gate and along the bridleway. We are now in Colwell Wood, a fine example of a deciduous woodland, golden in the autumn, green in the summer and, as the nearby farm suggests, a riot of bluebells in late spring. After a while the public bridleway, complete with instructional sign, takes you downhill past another sign to a house close to a pond. Continue onwards staying with the trend in the direction. For a few hundred yards it is a levellish path but eventually rises steadily only to fall again.

Honiton Hill

Tower Farm

A35 (T)

To Axminster

Colwell Wood

S OFFWELL

It is a sunken track here and, as you might guess, on a sunken track you sink! We certainly found it somewhat soft, enough for someone to suggest that Offwell Woods be renamed "Softwell Woods"! Fortunately at the bottom is a gateway with a crossroads of tracks. Go straight across; through the next gap in the hedge on the left is a more open vista of the valley. Should the need arise, there is a footpath on the left which goes directly back to Offwell but for this book we are going to continue down the pleasant hedged lane which drops down to a sewage treatment works.

Offwell Brook

Colwell

This is a point where several small streams all flow south eastwards. One, in fact, so keen that it runs across our track as we approach two signposts. Here we turn right and immediately cross two more small watercourses, the first by a tiny stone footbridge and the second by a wooden construction. Now we are in the midst of coniferous woodland.

These woods have several damp spots with a healthy population of frogs and newts. We picked one up to have a little look before carefully putting him back where we found him. It then occurred to us that this newt might well have rushed straight to the offices of "The Newts of the World" (Offwell edition) resulting in a newspaper headline claiming an exclusive Close Encounter of the Third Kind!

That was the good new(t)s! The bad new(t)s is that we had walked straight past the correct path, adding an unnecessary hill climb of several hundred yards to our walk! So be warned and take care here!

After crossing the two bridges, follow the path for about a hundred yards of uphill stuff, looking closely to the left for a small track which starts at a marshy spot. You should still be within earshot of the waters you've just crossed. There is a yellow arrow to point the way but it is set back and is easily missed!

Having located the arrow, follow this track which soon becomes a more definite thoroughfare, ignoring a path which leads steeply up into the darkness of the dense wood. The yellow marked way leads to a gateway and stile. Cross it and soon it drops down between a line of trees on a raised bank.

This is an opportunity to show your powers of physical agility as at one point the path is annexed by a couple of trees that you have to get past – just take the correct 'root'!

Very soon a muddy gateway by a small stream is met. Cross the stream and pass through the gate which has a yellow arrow to assure you that you are going the right way. There are three tracks here, the one which is required is straight ahead towards a house called 'Hoopers'.

At the end of this public footpath a metalled road is met. It is possible to take the path signposted just beyond the junction as a little detour, but we headed down the surfaced road to the left because we were late. Both reach the same point so if you go down the hill, Mill Lane, you will cross the stream and rise up to the other end of the, presumably more aesthetically pleasing, alternative path. Stay on Village Lane as it bends, climbing quite steeply to reach Colwell Barton.

Just past the bulk of its buildings, turn left and walk along the road for a few hundred yards. On the right is another public footpath which is well worth taking as it is a short-cut back to Offwell. However, along it there are more stiles to negotiate. After just two of them you find yourself above the tree-line but there are few views despite the elevation. Blame it on Kenhill Copse!

Fortunately the next gateway compensates as the great wooded north-facing slopes across the valley make a lovely scene. Down in the valley the circular object, which people with poor eyesight might imagine is a luxury swimming pool, is in fact the sewage works we passed earlier!

Follow the top of the field around into what appears to be a lane but instead of walking up it cross the stile on your left and another a little way beyond. (They often seem to come as two-packs!)

Ahead, beyond a few trees and on the hill, is Offwell. Keep up a similar height as you cross the field until, after about a hundred yards, a gap in the fence will be spied. Go through it and head downhill to a gateway with a stile. On crossing the latter go right, up the hill back to your vehicle – don't forget to congratulate your fellow stragglers on completing this 5 mile long safari!

⑩ From Beer to Eternity? Well, Almost Branscombe ...

It may well be a book of family walks but the first instruction is guaranteed to drive you to drink. Go to Beer! (That is the village, not the brew.) This little fishing village, lying in the lee of great chalk cliffs, on fine days catches more tourists than fish! It is a charming place in which to start a walk, the only problem being that it lies in a deep, steep hollow so the only way out is up!

Park in one of the car parks in the village. Head down the main street towards the beach. By the Anchor Inn, see the signpost marked "Branscombe 2m–Link to Coast Path" and turn right uphill (up Common Lane). Notice as you go the flint walls either side. It is obvious that modern man has made greater use of them than his bronze age predecessors ever did.

At the top of the steep hill, turn left, following the signpost to Branscombe Mouth 1⅔. The lane leads to a house but the track passes by it on the right. A little further on we pass a large car park on the right. (If you had to park in this cliff top car park, you can start the walk from here – but you will have to follow the beginning part at the end!)

The coast path swings down to the left of a caravan park. Go through a 'swing' stile and follow the faint track to the left of a hedge. The track becomes stony at the top before another field leads to a stile with additional 'doggy gate' (guillotine-style).

A well-defined track leads to another stile. Sea mist permitting, you will now have extensive views of Seaton Bay, Seaton seafront and the mouth of the River Axe. Keep with the track and follow a yellow arrow which leads to another yellow arrow. A little further on, at Beer Head, swing right towards yet another stile. As you cross it, to your left you might notice the almost vertical, steep cliffs before crossing yet another stile. Fortunately there is plenty of ugly barbed wire fence to deter you from accidentally wandering off the cliff which is over 450 feet high and almost vertical!

You should now have a good view of an unusual coastguard building with bungalow which will soon be passed. If, like on the day we walked here, visibility is not good, keep on along the path, passing (without crossing) a stile which actually leads to 'Branscombe Mouth'. There is a choice of routes offered but we

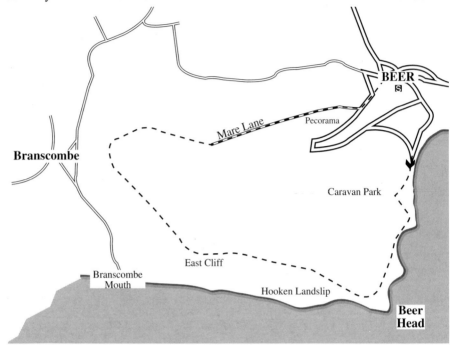

follow straight on up the hill towards 'Hooken Cliffs ¼m'. Pass the coastguard building then, at the next signpost, follow the Public Footpath sign to 'Branscombe Mouth ¾m'. A track leads up the middle of the field on very level, easy going, ground.

For some reason walking the coastline has become almost an obsession with walkers. Presumably it is the comforting thought that if they keep the sea to one side they can't possibly get lost! If you have counted how many people you have passed on the first half of this walk – compared to how many you will see on the second – you might conclude that the United Kingdom is peopled with folk dedicated to walking around its perimeter. Smugglers wouldn't stand a chance of being undetected today! Ironically this little stretch of coastline was notorious for the antics of Branscombe and Beer men. Of the latter, the greatest and most celebrated exponent was Jack Rattenbury who was so successful, and so admired, that he survived to draw a pension!

This route eventually leads to a stile at 'East Cliff'. Start walking gently downhill and look out for a stile in a fence on the right. Cross the stile. The path heads diagonally up the field towards a gate or, follow the left hand fence with views of Branscombe to the left and you should see a post with a yellow arrow on the left, in the gorse, followed shortly by another post with yellow arrow. Up on the right you will then see the gate. Head up to it, but don't go through it; walk along the track with the fence and hedge on your right.

The name of the walking game for the next half mile is to not drop down into the steep combe of Branscombe for what goes down will have to come back up again. There is a path of sorts but it fades and reappears so vigilance and an appreciation of the overall task in hand will serve you well. Bearing in mind that you will need to keep your height, follow these instructions as best you can.

The track keeps in the middle when the hedges widen off left and right. Go through the field exit (which has no gate) but is identified by an odd tree on the left and water troughs on the right. Keep on the same level, ignoring the wide track on the left, downhill. Go through a small gap on the right. Steer right of further downhill paths, keeping the fence on the right. Go through a gap ahead in the gorse with circular 'roundabout' gorse bush beyond, taking the left exit. Circle the gorse, keeping it on your right. The track goes into some bushes ahead. Go through, keeping the wood on your right. The track rises steeply uphill before joining a small track across the top. (If you have failed to spot this as a short cut, you will enter a wood and almost as soon as you are in it you will meet a track coming straight up the hill. Turn right and it will put you back on course.) You are at the top of Stockham's Hill.

At the very top, on the right, is a stile. Cross and go left along the the hedge. At the end of the field a signpost says we've come from Branscombe and points left to Beer Quarry, right to Mares Lane. Quite by chance, when we prepared this route, a mare in an adjacent field suddenly decided to come across and say hello. So this is why there is a photo of a mare at Mares Lane!

To the right of the sign is a stile with a yellow arrow. Either walk right to cross it or, if you have a puffed out pooch with you, the gap by the signpost allows easy access around, saving tired terriers extra exertions. From the stile head straight across the field to the next stile. You will find some additional steps on the far side to aid your landing! There is a choice of wide tracks – but we go straight ahead, not left or right. Keep on going.

Eventually we leave the fields behind to enter a hedge-banked lane, just before which is a public footpath sign in the hedge.

Ignore all gateways; keep right on to the end of the track. As you approach Beer you'll hear children enjoying Pecorama, glimpses of which will be seen through a hedge on the right. This is a tourist attraction which is principally noted for its model railways, one of which is large enough to take people on journeys around 'Beer Heights'. Avoid Pecorama car park on the left and take the road downhill to Beer.

At the end of Mare Lane (which has now become singular!) turn left down the road. At the bend, cross carefully and go down the public footpath beside a house called 'Four Winds'. At the bottom, cross the road to go down another path. Passing the cemetery on the left, turn left down the road back to the car park. (Unless your car is in the cliff car park in which case you will need to do the first part now!).

The last bit of this four mile long walk gives you the opportunity to get to the parts of Beer that other walks fail to reach – an appropriate place and an appropriate way in which to end *Ten Family Walks in East Devon* – hopefully in good spirits!